Understanding My Emotions

When I'm Surprised

Understanding My Emotions

When I'm Angry
When I'm Embarrassed
When I'm Happy
When I'm Lonely
When I'm Overwhelmed
When I'm Sad
When I'm Scared
When I'm Sorry
When I'm Surprised
When I'm Worried

Understanding My Emotions

When I'm Surprised

ALEXANDRA DALTON

**Understanding My Emotions
When I'm Surprised**

Copyright © 2016 by Village Earth Press, a division of Harding House Publishing. All rights reserved. No part of this publication may be reproduced or transmitted in any form or by any means, electronic or mechanical, including photocopying, recording, taping, or any information storage and retrieval system, without permission from the publisher.

Village Earth Press
Vestal, New York 13850
www.villageearthpress.com

First Printing
9 8 7 6 5 4 3 2 1

Series ISBN (paperback): 978-1-62524-440-6
ISBN (paperback): 978-1-62524-384-3
ebook ISBN: 978-1-62524-140-5
   Library of Congress Control Number: 2014941252

Author: Dalton, Alexandra.

Contents

To the Teacher or Parent   7

When I'm Surprised   8

Find Out More   42

Feeling Words   44

Index   46

Picture Credits   47

About the Author   48

To the Teacher or Parent

More than a hundred years ago, John Dewey insisted that the true purpose of schooling was not simply to teach children a trade but to train them in deeper habits of mind. Social-emotional learning builds on Dewey's theory further, suggesting that emotional skills are crucial to both academic performance and future success in life.

The research is definitive: emotional training is good for children! A recent study, reported in the *New York Times*, found that preschoolers who had even a single year of social-emotional training continued to perform better two years after they left the program; they were less aggressive and less anxious than children who hadn't participated in the program. Another study found that K-12 students who received some form of emotional instruction scored an average of 11 percentile points higher on standardized achievement tests. A similar study found a nearly 20 percent decrease in students' violent behaviors.

The goal of this series of books, UNDERSTANDING MY EMOTIONS, is to instill in young children a foundation of emotional intelligence. Use these books to help children learn to understand, identify, and regulate their emotions. Give them important tools that will serve them well for the rest of their lives!

When I'm Surprised

Every day I have lots and lots of feelings—and so do you!

Our bodies feel many different things.

We feel cold when we play in the snow.

We feel hot on summer days at the beach.

We feel hungry when our tummies are empty.

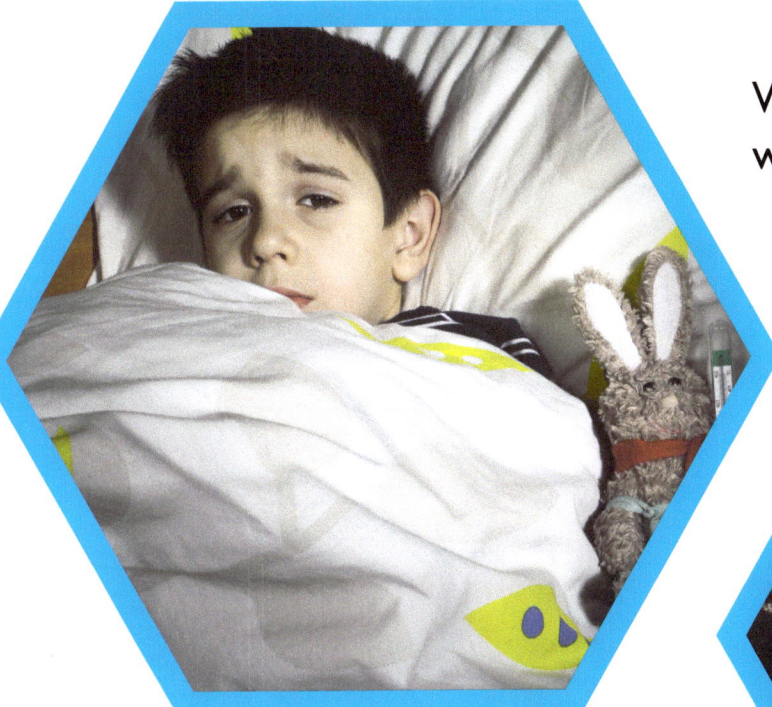

We feel sore and yucky when we're sick.

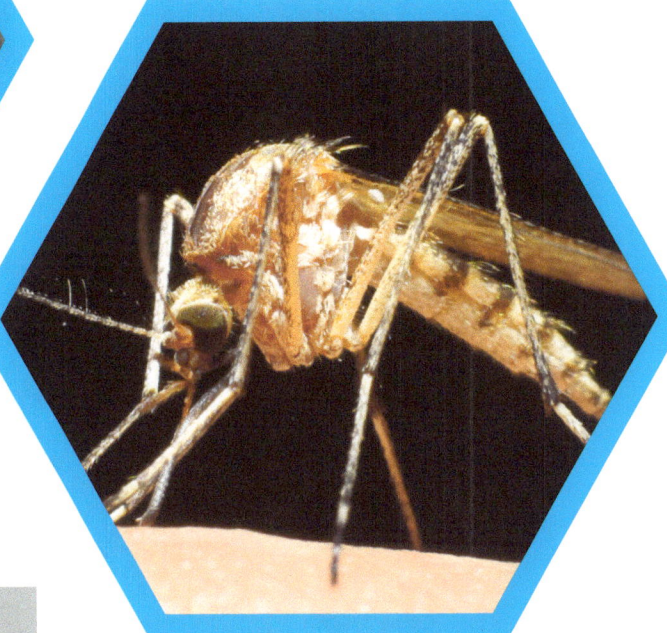

We feel itchy when a mosquito bites us.

And we feel sleepy when we're tired.

We have other feelings too. These feelings happen inside our heads. They're called emotions.

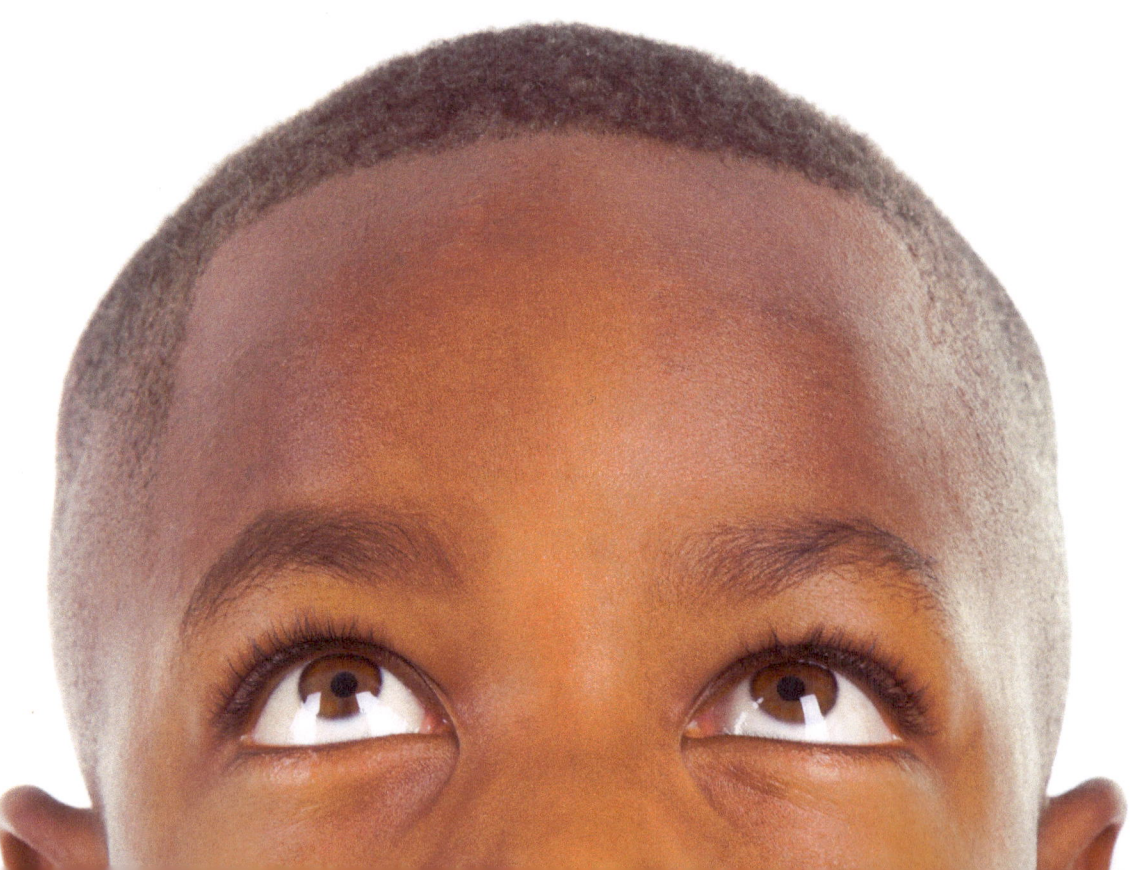

We have many different emotions. Sad and happy, scared and angry are all emotions. There are lots of other emotions too.

Some emotions are fun to feel.

It's fun to feel so happy you can't help smiling.

It's fun to feel excited because something wonderful happened.

It's fun to feel friendly when you get a new babysitter.

Other emotions aren't fun to feel.

Feeling bored when there's nothing to do isn't fun.

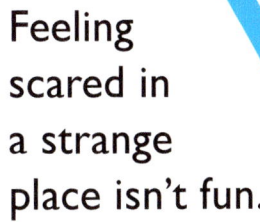

Feeling scared in a strange place isn't fun.

Feeling sad is never fun at all!

Another emotion is surprise. Surprise is what we feel when something happens that we weren't expecting.

Surprise can be a lot of fun—like when your grandma gives you a gift just because she loves you, when it's not even your birthday.

But sometimes surprise isn't so much fun—like when all of a sudden you fall off your bike.

Surprise is a feeling that happens inside your head. Maybe that doesn't seem to make sense. After all, the present from your grandma isn't inside your head. You didn't fall down on your bike inside your head!

But it's the FEELING that happens in your head. When something happens that you didn't expect, your brain makes the feeling called surprise.

Your brain is inside your head. Your brain is a round, wrinkly thing. It's the part of you that thinks. You use your brain every time you have an idea. You use it when you learn. You use it when you daydream. Your brain does many, many wonderful things.

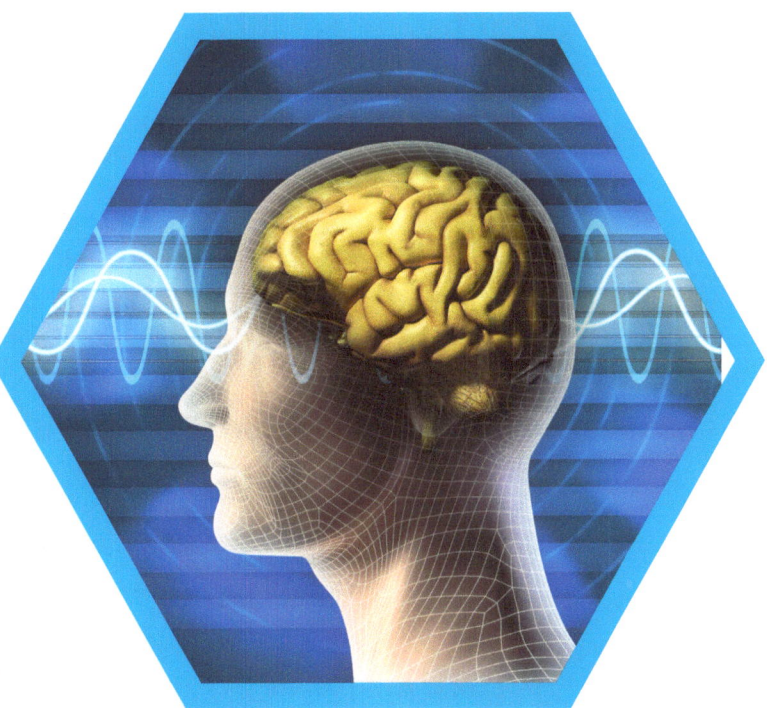

Your brain tells the rest of your body what to do. It's the boss! Your brain has lots of parts inside it—and each part controls a different part of your body.

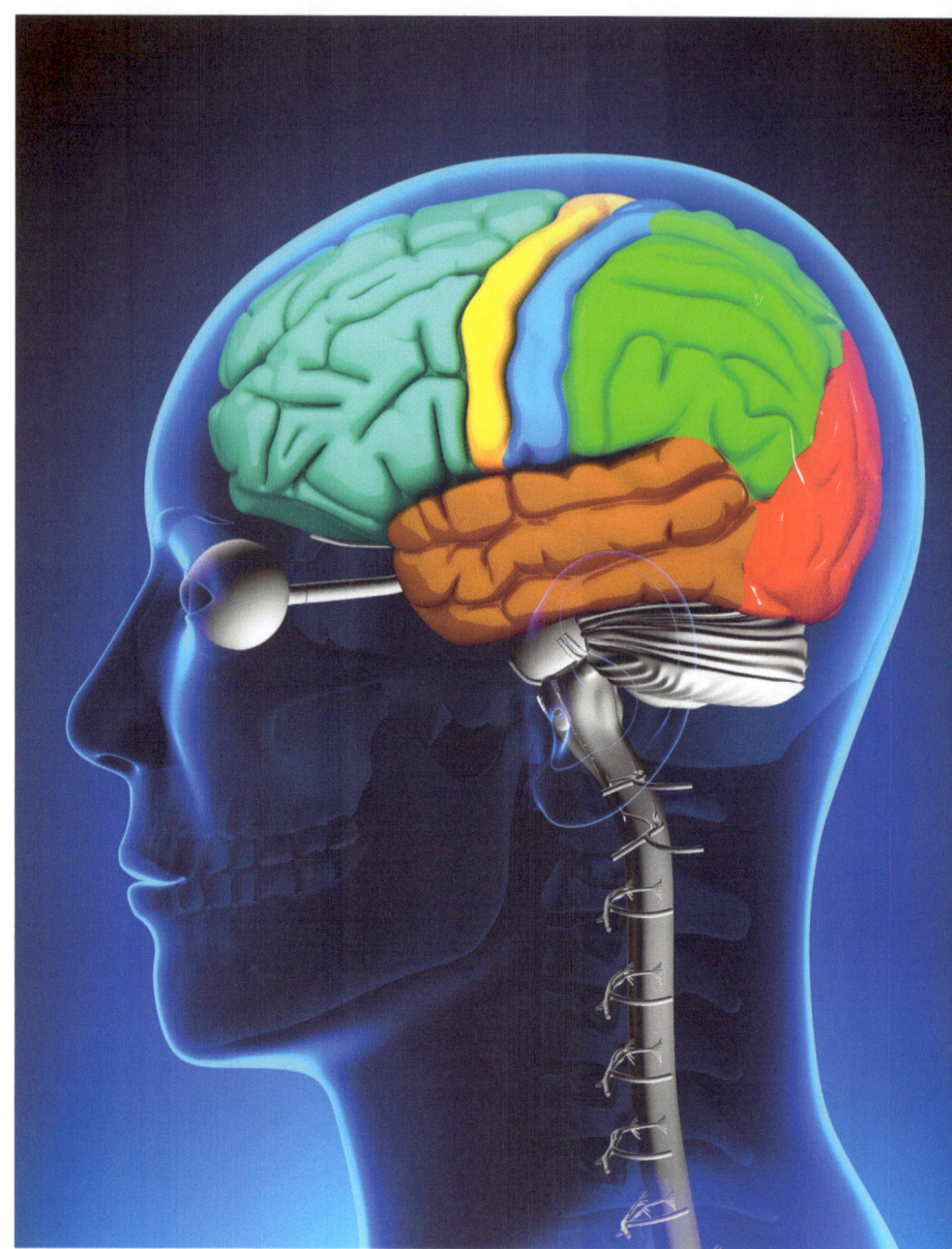

One part of your brain is connected to your eyes and ears. You use your eyes and ears to see and hear—but you also use your brain. Without your brain, you wouldn't be able to see or hear.

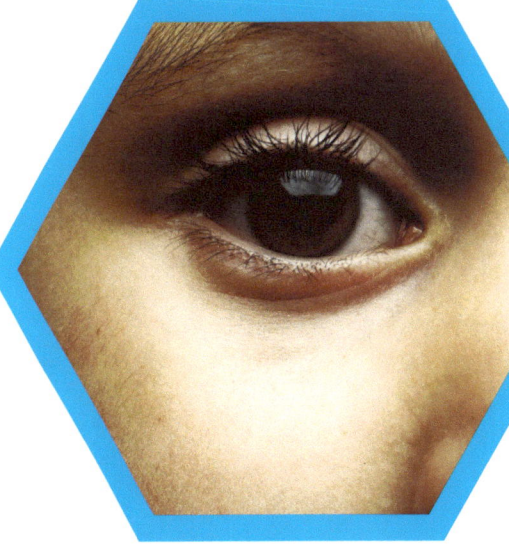

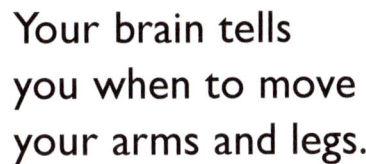

Your brain tells you when to move your arms and legs.

You use your mouth to talk to your friend—and your ears to listen to her. But it's your brain that tells your mouth what to say. It understands the words your friend says to you.

Your brain is also what makes all the feelings called emotions.

When something sad happens—like your best friend moving to a new city—your brain makes the sadness you feel.

The sad feeling in your brain might make your mouth turn down. It can make you cry.

When something good happens—like getting a new puppy—your brain makes the happiness you feel. This time, your mouth turns up!

And when your friend jumps out at you from behind a tree, your brain makes the feeling we call surprise!

Some people love to feel surprised. Surprises make them happy.

Other people don't like to feel surprised. Even good surprises can make them feel a little scared.

Feeling surprised is a little different from most of the other emotions we have. When you're sad or happy, that feeling will stick around for a while. But sometimes surprise only lasts an instant! If someone jumps out at you and says, "Boo!" you feel surprised right then—but you're not still feeling surprised an hour later.

Surprise usually turns into something else— another feeling—very quickly. It can turn into laughter, like when a clown jumps out and does something funny.

But what if it's not a clown that jumps at you? What if it's a really big dog instead? Then your surprise might turn into fear!

If it turns out the dog is friendly, though, your surprise might turn into friendly, glad feelings.

If someone shoves you on the playground, you feel surprised at first—and then you might feel angry.

Sometimes I'm one of the people who like surprises. Surprises make me laugh. They turn into excited, happy feelings. Without any surprises, life would be pretty boring.

But other times I'm one of those people who really don't like surprises! I don't like the surprises that make me feel scared—or sad—or angry.

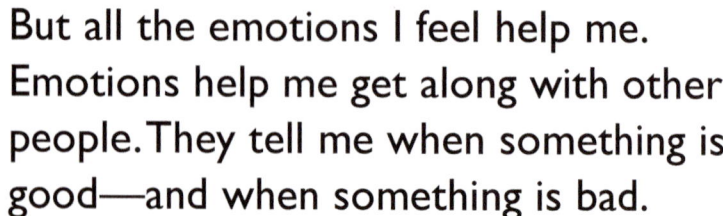

But all the emotions I feel help me. Emotions help me get along with other people. They tell me when something is good—and when something is bad.

Surprise helps me, like all the other emotions do. Surprise is like a flag going up. It's a signal telling me to pay attention!

It's a message that says, "Watch out! Be careful!"

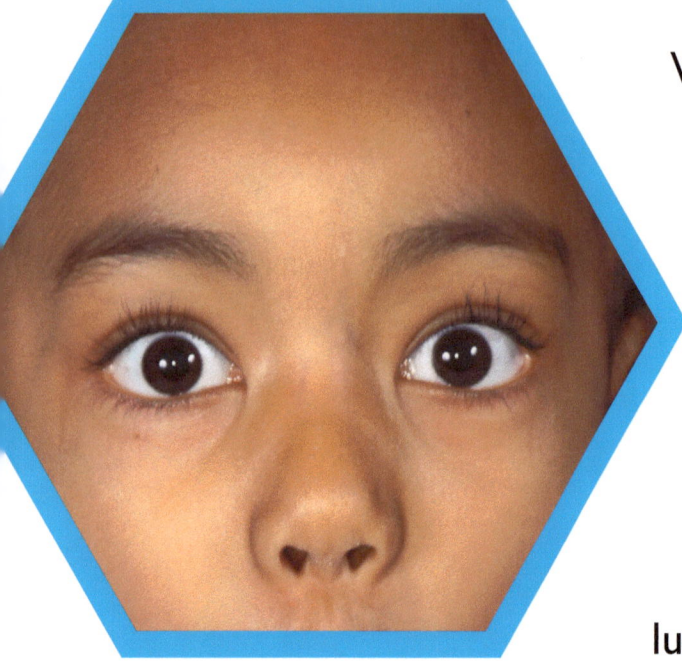

When I'm surprised, right away my brain sends out messages to the rest of my body. My brain tells my eyes to get big, so I can see what's happening.

My brain tells my body to breathe in a little extra air. The air has oxygen, which goes into my lungs. My lungs are like sacs inside my chest that fill up with air. My lungs get the oxygen out of the air. Then my lungs send the oxygen to the rest of my body. The oxygen gets my body ready to do whatever it needs to do.

I need oxygen all the time—but I might need more if I have to run away from something scary! That's why we gasp sometimes when we're surprised. We're sucking in a little extra oxygen.

My blood carries the oxygen from my lungs to my muscles. Muscles are like big stretchy rubber bands fastened to my bones. My muscles move my arms and legs. They help me run or push or jump.

Surprise makes my heart beat faster and harder. My heart is a pump made out of muscle. It's in my chest too, along with my lungs. My heart pumps blood through my whole body. The harder and faster my heart beats, the more blood gets sent to my muscles and the rest of my body. Now my muscles are ready to do whatever needs doing!

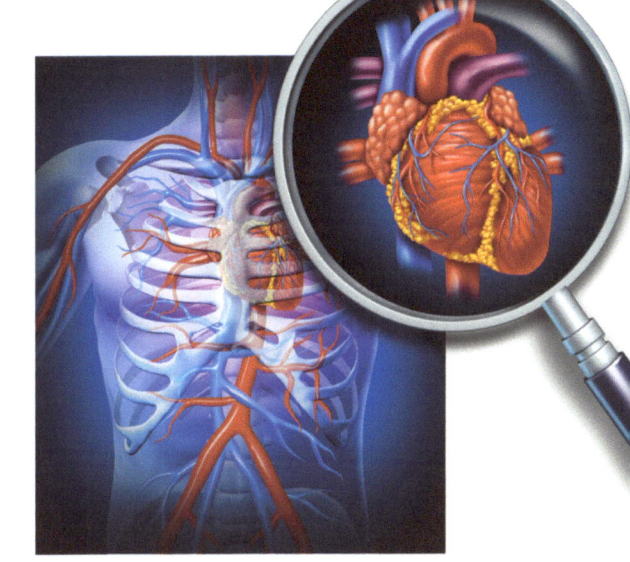

Surprise gets me ready for whatever comes next. Maybe it gets me ready to run away from something scary. Or I might be ready to push back when someone tries to shove me. Or I might start to laugh!

33

People who don't like surprise might feel as though their life is out of control when they have too many surprises in a row. Things they don't expect keep happening. They can't make plans. They feel like they don't have any control. That makes them feel scared. It can make them feel stressed.

Stress is what happens when we have too many things happening all at once. Our bodies are trying to handle it all—but it's hard! Even people who like surprises can feel stressed if they have too many surprises all at once.

Even good surprises can make us stressed. All that excitement is just too much! When we're stressed, we might have a stomachache or a headache.

We might cry more easily.

It might be hard to go to sleep at night.

When I feel like there are too many surprises in my life, I can do something that will help me cope. There are things I can do to take away some of my stress.

Laughing is one of the best ways to get rid of stress. Doing something fun with my family or my friends gives me reasons to laugh. Laughing makes me feel better. So when there are too many surprises in my life, laughing with my family and my friends helps me cope. It makes me remember that surprises don't have to be such a big deal. It helps me relax.

Taking time to be quiet is another way I can handle too many surprises. If I sit down and read a book for a while, I don't feel so stressed. That's something that helps me relax.

Maybe something else will work better for you. You could go for a walk with your dog—or just sit and watch a sunset. Do something quiet that you like doing!

There's another good way to keep from being stressed by surprise. You can turn surprise into curiosity. Curiosity is another emotion we have. When we wonder about something and want to learn more, we're feeling curious. So instead of feeling scared by a surprise, you could take a closer look at it.

You can try to find out something new. Maybe you could use the Internet to look for answers.

You could ask your mom or dad to take you to the library.

If you're curious about something, you could ask your teacher to help you understand. Curiosity helps you learn new things.

You might figure out how to deal with a problem. Or you might find out that something you thought was scary isn't so scary after all!

You might get a new idea—and make something wonderful!

So the next time you feel surprised? Here are some things you can do so surprises don't scare you and make you stressed:

- Laugh. Turn the surprise into laughter.
- Have fun with your friends or family.
- Relax. Do something quiet that you like to do.
- Be curious. Learn something new!

Life is full of surprises. Things we don't expect will always happen—so we might as well enjoy them. Just think how boring it would be if there were no surprises!

Find Out More

You can learn more about your emotions by going online and checking out these websites. Some of the sites have videos you can watch or games you can play. You could also read the other books in this series to find out more about feelings—or you could go to your library and see if you can find the books listed on the next page. There's a lot more you can learn about surprise and other feelings!

On the Internet

It's My Life: Emotions
pbskids.org/itsmylife/emotions

KidsHealth: Feelings
kidshealth.org/kid/feeling

Model Me: Faces and Emotions
www.modelmekids.com/emotions_dvd.html

In Books

Aliki. *Feelings*. New York: Greenwillow Books, 2007.

Curtis, Jamie Lee. *Today I Feel Silly: And Other Moods That Make My Day.* New York: HarperCollins, 2007.

Freyman, Saxton. *How Are You Peeling?* Danbury, Conn.: Scholastic, 2004.

Krueger, David. *What Is a Feeling?* Seattle, Wash.: Parenting Press, 2013.

Rotner, Shelley. *Lots of Feelings*. Minneapolis, Minn.: Millbrook Press, 2003.

Snow, Todd. *Feelings to Share from A to Z.* Lake Elmo, Minn.: Maren Green, 2007.

Feeling Words

Feeling embarrassed is just one of our feelings. There are many other feelings, and many words we use to describe them. Here are some of them.

Proud

Scared

Shy

Sorry

Embarrassed

Bored

Index

An index is a way you can quickly find something inside a book. The numbers tell you exactly what page to turn to if you want to find that word.

angry 13, 27, 29
arm 21, 33
attention 30

babysitter 14
bike 17–18
blood 33
body 10, 20, 32–34
bored 15, 28, 41
brain 19–23, 32
breathe 32

clown 26–27
cold 10
control 34
curiosity 38–39
cry 22, 35

dad 38
daydream 19

dog 27, 37
ear 21
emotion 12–16, 22, 26, 30, 38
eyes 21, 32

feelings 9, 12, 15, 18–19, 22–23, 26–28, 38
friend 21–23, 36, 40

gift 17
grandma 17–18

happy 13–14, 24, 26, 28
head 12, 18–19
headaches 35
hot 10
hungry 10

idea 19, 39

laughter 26, 28, 33, 36, 40
learn 19, 38–40
leg 21, 33

mom 38
muscle 33

playground 27
puppy 23

quiet 37, 40

sad 13, 15, 22, 26, 29
scared 13, 15, 25, 29, 34, 38
sick 11
signal 30
sleep 11, 35
stress 34–36, 37–38, 40

Picture Credits

p. 8: © Sam74100 | Dreamstime.com
p. 9: © Sam74100 | Dreamstime.com
p. 10: © David Hanlon | Dreamstime.com, © Darren Green | Dreamstime.com, © Monkey Business Images | Dreamstime.com
p. 11: © Deyangeorgiev | Dreamstime.com, © Mircea Costina | Dreamstime.com, © Mocker | Dreamstime.com
p. 12: © Sam74100 | Dreamstime.com
p. 13: © Anna Szon | Dreamstime.com
p. 14: © Mohamed Osama | Dreamstime.com, © Canettistock | Dreamstime.com, © Jamie Wilson | Dreamstime.com
p. 16: © Jodielee | Dreamstime.com, © | Dreamstime.com, © Maen Zayyad | Dreamstime.com
p. 17: © Kenishirotie | Dreamstime.com, © Susan Sheldon | Dreamstime.com
p. 18: © Sam74100 | Dreamstime.com
p. 19: © Corina Rosu | Dreamstime.com, © Andreus | Dreamstime.com
p. 20: © Decade 3D | Dreamstime.com
p. 21: © Kyle Simpson | Dreamstime.com, © Michael Gray | Dreamstime.com, © Monkey Business Images | Dreamstime.com
p. 22: © Sparkla | Dreamstime.com, © Yelena Rodriguez | Dreamstime.com
p. 23: © Goce Risteski | Dreamstime.com, © Auremar | Dreamstime.com
p. 24: © Waraphon Banchobdi | Dreamstime.com, © Pixies | Dreamstime.com, © Ariwasabi | Dreamstime.com, © Tony Livingston | Dreamstime.com
p. 25: © Julien Grondin | Dreamstime.com, © Agenturfotographin | Dreamstime.com, © Stephen Day | Dreamstime.com, © Ookosun | Dreamstime.com

p. 26: © Dreamzdesigner | Dreamstime.com © Lisa F. Young | Dreamstime.com
p. 27: Eichenluft © | Dreamstime.com, © Zoran Mijatov | Dreamstime.com, © Cheryl Casey | Dreamstime.com
p. 28 © Sam74100 | Dreamstime.com
p. 29: © Sam74100 | Dreamstime.com
p. 30: © PixelRobot | Dreamstime.com
p. 31: © Sam74100 | Dreamstime.com
p. 32: © Patricia Marks | Dreamstime.com, © DarrenW | Dreamstime.com
p. 33: © Linda Bucklin | Dreamstime.com, © Skypixel | Dreamstime.com, © Sam74100 | Dreamstime.com
p. 34: © Yanlev | Dreamstime.com
p. 35: © Deyangeorgiev | Dreamstime.com, © Valentino2 | Dreamstime.com, © Xiebiyun | Dreamstime.com
p. 36: © Spotmatik | Dreamstime.com, © Diego Vito Cervo | Dreamstime.com
p. 37: © Sam74100 | Dreamstime.com, © Sonya Etchison | Dreamstime.com, © Alina Shilzhyavichyute | Dreamstime.com
p. 38: © Irina Papoyan | Dreamstime.com, © Lifede | Dreamstime.com © Photoeuphoria | Dreamstime.com
p. 39: © Pavolova Sakova | Dreamstime.com, © Monkey Business Images | Dreamstime.com, © Christin Gasner | Dreamstime.com
p. 41: © Sam74100 | Dreamstime.com
p. 44: Fotolia: © Fasphotographic, © Cantor Pannato, © Andres Rodriguez, © Gabriel Blaj, © Moodboard Premium, © Halfpoint
p. 45: Fotolia: © Cantor Pannato, © Blend Images, © Zhekos, © Olly, © Wavebreak Media Micro; © Serrnovik | Dreamstime.com

About the Author

Alexandra Dalton was a teacher, and now she is a writer. When she was a teacher, she helped her students talk about their feelings. She knows that it's hard work sometimes to talk about our feelings—but she knows we feel better and we get along with each other better when we can use our words to talk about how we feel. Alexandra has three children. She also has a dog and a cat and four goats. She lives in New York State.

www.ingramcontent.com/pod-product-compliance
Lightning Source LLC
Chambersburg PA
CBHW061359090426
42743CB00002B/73